Day Lasts Forever:

Selected Poems of Mario dell'Arco

translated from Romanesco by Marc Alan Di Martino

 WORLD POETRY

Day Lasts Forever: Selected Poems of Mario dell'Arco
Copyright © Marcello Fagiolo dell'Arco / Fondo Mario dell'Arco, 2024
English translation copyright © Marc Alan Di Martino, 2024

First Edition, First Printing, 2024
ISBN 978-1-954218-27-7

World Poetry Books
New York, NY
www.worldpoetrybooks.com

Available to the trade through Asterism Books
Distributed in the UK and Europe by Turnaround Publisher Services
Subscriptions and standing orders available directly from the publisher

Library of Congress Control Number: 2024943193

Cover image: Renato Guttuso, *Cactus*, 1967. © 2024 Artists Rights Society (ARS), New York / SIAE, Rome.

Frontispiece portrait (by Eugen Drăguțescu) and author photograph are printed with the permission of Fondo Mario dell'Arco.

Cover design by Andrew Bourne
Typesetting by Don't Look Now
Printed in Lithuania by BALTO Print

A publisher of exceptional translations of poetry from a broad range of languages and traditions, bringing the work of modern masters, emerging voices, and pioneering innovators from around the world to English-language readers in affordable trade editions, World Poetry Books is a 501(c)(3) nonprofit and charitable organization founded in 2017 in New York City, affiliated with the Humanities Institute and the Translation Program at the University of Connecticut (Storrs), and a member of the Community of Literary Magazines and Presses (CLMP).

Contents

Maturing Towards Infancy:
The Life and Poetry of Mario dell'Arco *ix*

from *Red Inside* (1946)
Sloth *21*
Night School *23*
St. Peter's Square *25*
Tasso's Oak *27*

from *Paper Star* (1947)
Via dei Cappellari *29*
Propaganda *31*
The Scarecrow *33*

from *Tormarancio* (1950)
When It's Time *35*

from *A Strip of Sun* (1951)
Puppet Theater *37*

from *How I Like It* (1953)
Spruce *39*
How I Like It *41*
Sundial *43*

from *Rome 18 Poems* (1956)
The Steps at Aracoeli *45*

from *The Swan* (1957)
Waning Moon *47*
Sunflower *49*

from *Homage to Aesop* (1958)
Diffidence *51*
Jove's Advice *53*

The Collector of Fables   55
Roman Nature   57

from *Heads or Tails?* (1960)
Heads or Tails?   59

from *A Cradle in My Chest* (1961)
An Unsure Step   61
Bated Breath   63
Day Lasts Forever   65
All of Gold   67
Always a Cradle   69

from *Living Green Dead Green* (1962)
Ice Cream Cone   71

from *Martial for a Month* (1963)
12. [You ask how green my garden grows.]   73

from *Poems 1942-1967* (1967)
Nuts, or Not Nuts?   75
Wine and Poetry   77
I Built a Wall   79

from *And I Drink Flowers and Wine* (1968)
Genzano Wine   81

from *Tiber River Anthology* (1970)
IV. [I, Dr., Prof., freelance docent]   89
X. [HERE (at last!) LIES]   91
XI. [At last God has recalled]   93
XVI. [The walls have fallen in around]   95

from *Hunting Diary* (1971)
A Trill Within   97
Warbler   99
A Beautiful Death   101

from *Let Me Have Some Fun, or Martial for Another Month* (1972)

6. [A hundred flatterers hawk around Katz's]   103
8. [Again painting still lifes:]   105
15. [Are these epigrams any good? Who knows?]   107
23. [You fress like a hog—loud, face smeared]   109
26. [A pair of thrushes picked]   111

from *Four Corners* (1973)

The Illiterate Fish   113
Star Hunter   115
A Slice of Watermelon   117

from *Shadowplay* (1974)

Like a Hare   119

from *Poems 1950-1975* (1976)

Dead Branches   121

from *Arciroma* (1978)

The Colosseum Is a Shell   123
Nero's Tomb   125
Watermelon   127
Enough (or Not?)   129

from *Cats* (1980)

I, Cat   131

from *Flora* (1981)

The Apple   133

from *Solo* (1982)

Solo   135

from *Cats, Who Wants Cats?* (1985)

The Ash-Cat   141
The Sand-Colored Cat   143

from *Triumph of Blue* (1985)
Fear of Solitude   *145*

from *Crossing the Bridge* (1986)
A Cob Thick with Stars   *147*

from *Odd-Numbered Angel (1990)*
Campo de' Fiori   *149*

from *Roma Romae* (1991)
Blackbird   *151*
Spiral Staircase   *153*

Notes to the Poems   *155*

Acknowledgments   *159*

Maturing Towards Infancy:
The Life and Poetry of Mario dell'Arco

In 2003, after eight years in New York City, I threw in the towel and moved in with my aunt in our family apartment in Rome. I told myself I was on sabbatical. I was there to find myself, or write a book, or at least some new poems. Or meet someone. *Or die trying.* In the meantime, I used those seemingly endless days to improve my Italian and trawl the still-plentiful secondhand bookshops in the Campo Marzio, burning through my fisherman's sandals on the blistering paving stones during the hottest summer in living memory.

It was in one of those bookshops, wedged between Campo de' Fiori and Piazza Navona, that I stumbled upon a used volume of Mario dell'Arco's *Poesie Romanesche*. I was already familiar with the major Romanesco—or Roman dialect—poets, members of a tradition largely inaugurated by Giuseppe Gioachino Belli. Belli, a contemporary of Gogol and Poe, wrote more than two thousand sonnets in the spoken language of the poor, uneducated Romans of his time. They make for challenging reading today. His project was a kind of total representation of his world, comparable to Balzac's Paris and Joyce's Dublin. He left no cobblestone unturned in his quest to record even the most vulgar utterance of the Roman underclasses. He gave a voice to the powerless and marginalized. He satirized the still-mighty Catholic Church. He wrote highly explicit poems, beloved by translators, about the infamous prostitute Santaccia—or, *St. Bad Girl*. He may or may not have met Keats. His footprint on Romanesco poetry is gargantuan and indelible.

Belli died in 1863. Many poets appeared in his wake: Cesare Pascarella, who wrote a verse-novel called *La Scoperta de l'America* (*The Discovery of America*); Crescenzo Del Monte, who penned sonnets in Giudaico-Romanesco (the dialect of the Jewish ghetto, liberally peppered with Hebrew) and even translated Belli from one dialect to the other; Carlo Alberto Salustri—a.k.a. Trilussa—certainly the most popular Romanesco poet of the post-Belli era, known for his "re-modernized" Aesopian fables showcasing razor-sharp social satire. Of course, there are many others, and the Romanesco sonnet is still something of a commonplace in Rome (my aunt owned a Romanesco cookbook by the beloved actor Aldo Fabrizi; all the recipes were written as sonnets). After Trilussa (d. 1950), however, the tradition begins to trickle away. This may in part be due to a general waning of dialects across the peninsula. The era of television had begun, and Italian was becoming a truly homogeneous language. Enter Mario dell'Arco.

Mario Fagiolo, who wrote under the pen name Mario dell'Arco, was born in Rome on March 12, 1905, in Via dell'Orso, not far from Piazza Navona. Trained as an architect before the war, he was paying homage to his other life: "Archi-tect, arch, dell'Arco." "Warning!" dell'Arco wrote, "if you see me on the scaffolding of a house under construction ... I'm Mario Fagiolo. If, instead, you see me belly up in the field, tickling the clouds with a blade of grass between my teeth, make no mistake: I'm Mario dell'Arco." From the publication of his first book, *Taja ch'è rosso* in 1946, dell'Arco was hailed as an innovative voice not only among his fellow dialect poets, but on the Italian literary scene in general. He was reviewed favorably by Pier Paolo Pasolini, with whom he would later compile an anthology of Italian dialect poetry of the first half of the twentieth century, and by Leonardo Sciascia, among other influential critics of the time. Dell'Arco published nearly sixty books—one a year—over the next five decades: slim volumes with sometimes as few as nineteen short poems, illustrated by various artists. There are the *Octaves* (1948), which deal more formally with historical concerns such as plague, gang warfare, and the Sack of Rome, but they are outnumbered by more playful titles like *Homage to Aesop, Martial for a Month, The Gospel of Mario dell'Arco,* and *Bacchus in Frascati*. After a long, self-imposed exile in his father's hometown of Genzano (one of the Roman Castles, famous for its bread), dell'Arco died on April 4, 1996. The last poem his collected works is appropriately titled "The Bread of Genzano."

Dell'Arco's poetry is marked by its bittersweet, almost jaded stance, a hallmark of the Roman attitude towards life (and death). The critic Pietro Paolo Trompeo astutely identified dell'Arco's Romanesco as being "not merely in his syntax or his vocabulary, but in his psychology." In today's Italy, dialects are mostly the stuff of one's barely literate or illiterate grandparents (yes, they still exist), or of fanatical political separatists. Roman youths still talk tough as they always have, but they can no longer boast more than a few words that would send a *forastiero*—out-of-towner—to the dictionary. Roman Jews have a few more in their arsenal—imported mainly from Hebrew, ancient and modern—but even they aren't likely conversant with their greatest poet, Crescenzo Del Monte. Mario dell'Arco's major achievement was a lyrical Romanesco. Gone from his work are the nasty, brutish accents of Belli; gone, too, are the sonnets, an extremely popular form of Romanesco poetic expression well into the twenty-first century. Dell'Arco vetoed his early sonnets from republication, perhaps in an attempt to recast himself in a modernist light. After World War II he wrote, "No more sonnets. Concise poems, almost epigrams." We are left with hundreds of six- to ten-line poems of an inward intensity and lyricism that one might compare to the works of Giuseppe Ungaretti, or even the American poet Samuel Menashe.

The poet wrote profusely about his native Rome—its streets, its monuments, its fauna—in poems ranging from the whimsical to the elegiac, from the socially conscious to the theologically argumentative. (The latter theme is evident in his 1983 book *The Gospel According to Mario dell'Arco*.) He translated Catullus, Horace, and Martial into Romanesco by reimagining their epigrams, teleporting them two thousand years into the future to speak again in Mario dell'Arco's accent. He wrote a *Spoon River*–inspired collection called *Tiber River Anthology*, after the river of his birthplace, where he and his infant son lie buried among the epitaphs.

Dell'Arco's father had owned a succession of taverns in Rome, where he sold wine from his native Genzano. In his long poem "And I Drink Flowers and Wine," he makes the senses tingle: "I sacrifice wine to the god of wine, / violet-colored *cesanese*, / crushed amethyst that burns the throat." By the end of the poem, the speaker has been entombed beneath the vine in yet another self-burial:

> Earth, up to my eyes—yet I see the wine,
> the new wine, and it makes no difference—
> *cesanese, trebbiano,* or *malvasia*—
> the taste of earth prevails and seals my lips.

Reading Mario dell'Arco, I am often reminded of the Yiddish poet Avrom Sutzkever's dictum: "This is poetry: a touch so gentle / no one should see a fingerprint." Dell'Arco's best work—in stark contrast to that of Belli and the other Romanesco poets—is of such a lightness.

> Heads or tails? Tossed
> way too high, the moon got lost
> glued to the pitch-black breast of night,
> a sleight-of-hand. You'll never know
> if it was heads or tails now.

What begins with the flip of a coin ends with the speaker marveling at the full moon as it brims with ancestral human uncertainty. But in dell'Arco, this uncertainty is not dread or existential angst; it is childlike wonder. Or, as Bruno Schulz put it, a "maturing towards infancy." Much of dell'Arco's work seems to me a fulfillment of this idea: we see the poet licking an ice cream cone, picking his teeth with a blade of grass, gazing up at a flawless blue sky, trading places with a mangy cat. The persona is that of the jaded dreamer, one who has lived—and lost—so much that all he has room for are marginal, almost trivial pleasures. We might imagine him as the subject of Marc Chagall's early painting, "The Poet Reclining": lying on the grass, jacket balled up beneath his head, blue sky above, lost forever in a dream.

Many of dell'Arco's most moving poems are about the loss of family—always there as an intangible presence, so often on the receiving end of the pronoun *you*, as in the poem "Always a Cradle," written "for my unborn daughter":

> Always, always a cradle
> rocking within me.
>   As the swarm of thoughts swells
> and sleep slips away
> I sing *rock-a-bye*,
> and I fall asleep, too
> right next to you.

Dell'Arco enjoyed institutional recognition late in his career. His eightieth birthday was celebrated on the Campidoglio in Rome, and at ninety he was given honorary citizenship by the town of Genzano. It is perhaps surprising, then, that he has fallen into near-obscurity a quarter century after his death. In the almost two decades that I have been reading, translating, and thinking about dell'Arco's work, no more than a handful of the many poets and translators I have spoken with have so much as registered his name. Individual poems have appeared in many languages, including Vietnamese, but translations of his work into English are so scarce that I had never come across any when I published my first versions in the *Journal of Italian Translation* in 2010. Further research has since yielded a few, mostly irretrievable on the Internet, confined to paperbound anthologies from the 1960s or published in special-interest journals of a scholarly bent. The only contemporary translations available online—besides my own—are by Luigi Bonaffini, editor of the *Journal of Italian Translation,* published on his website Italian Dialect Poetry.

Crucially, there has never been a book-length selection of dell'Arco's work available to readers of English. As a student of Italian, I relied heavily on facing-page translations to decipher Dante, Montale, and other Italian poets I wanted to read well before I was able to approach them head-on in the original. The aim of this volume is to introduce Mario dell'Arco to a fresh readership, one his poems have never had before.

That said, the poems in this volume represent an entirely personal selection of his work. There has been no attempt to be representative of his oeuvre, nor could there have been in so few pages. I've left out the octaves, for example, and confined myself to the concise epigrammatic poems. I've perhaps over-represented certain themes (hunting, wine) at the cost of others (theology, nature). I am to blame for any lacunae. My hope is that something of dell'Arco's accent will remain intact—his *psychology*—notwithstanding the shaky bridge between mid-twentieth-century Romanesco and early twenty-first century American English. I sought to mimic the rich internal music of his poems without sacrificing their epigrammatic punch lines, which often led to my being tongue-tied amid the lyrical chaos. Then, of course, there are the Romanesco words themselves, with their innumerable shades of meaning and allusion. How are they best rendered in English? American vernacular is felicitously hodgepodge, and finding equivalents can be enjoyable work in itself. Dell'Arco described his versions of Martial as "encounters" between the ancient Latin poet and the modern Roman one. He liked to mix it up and see what worked. Perhaps every such encounter is an experiment in the possibilities of literary translation, testing the limits of invention.

Rome, August 2021. I'm standing in front of the sun-drenched Colosseum—as I have a hundred times before—explaining to friends that the name refers not to the spectacular amphitheater in whose shadow we are standing but to the long-vanished Colossus of Nero that once stood at our feet. In that moment I recall the words of Mario dell'Arco:

> Forget about putting your ear
> to the Colosseum, friend.
>   The gladiator's winning cry,
> the bulls' stampede,

> the music of the choir,
> the whining *Te Deum*. In the end
> it's noise I alone can hear.

Two thousand years of history condensed into seven lines. "The Colosseum Is a Shell" collapses the distance between past and present; hold your ear up to the poem and all the glories and excesses of the ancient city flood into your consciousness. I know of no better way to travel through time than in the sleek chariot of a poem.

Marc Alan Di Martino

Portrait of Mario dell'Arco by Eugen Drăguțescu (1975)

Day Lasts Forever

Taja ch'è rosso (1946)

Accidia

  Chi più de me? Me sdraio in mezzo ar prato
tra papaveri e bocche-de-leone,
e me sento er padrone der creato.
Ma er celo è troppo limpido:
pesco una macedonia ner pacchetto
e fo nasce una nuvola,
così domani piove e resto a letto.

from *Red Inside* (1946)

Sloth

    Who more than me? Lying on the grass
surrounded by poppies and snapdragons,
I feel myself the lord of all creation.
The sky is too blue, though:
I fish a smoke from the pack
and blow a cloud above my head
so tomorrow it rains, and I can stay in bed.

Scola serale

    Er celo è la lavagna,
la luna è la maestra; e cor gessetto
disegna lo Scorpione,
la Bilancia, el Leone.
    In mezzo a la campagna
un «ci, i: cì» solitario; l'ucelletto,
invece d'annà a letto,
se studia er silabbario.

Night School

      The sky is the blackboard.
Miss Moon, with a piece of chalk,
traces Scorpio, Libra, Leo.
      The field comes alive with talk:
a lone *pee-p, pee-p!*—a fledgling.
Instead of going to bed
it's learning the alphabet.

Piazza San Pietro

Er colonnato ha messo le radice
tutt'intorno a la piazza,
sotto a un celo che sguazza de vernice.
E le funtane, visto er tempo bello,
so' uscite cor pennacchio sur cappello.

St. Peter's Square

    Columns rooted like trees
wreathe the square beneath
a turquoise-splattered sky.
The fountains, given the weather,
adorn their hats with a feather.

La quercia der Tasso

Esce su la stampella
e poi se ferma co' la mano stesa,
a un passo da la chiesa,
come una poverella.
E mentre se fa notte
ecco er vento, e je tira
le prime foje gialle sporche rotte
che pareno cartine da una lira.

Tasso's Oak

    She walks on crutches, halts,
withered hand outstretched
like a beggar before the church.
Night falls as wind whips, strips
off her leaves—rotten, faded, torn
as one-lira banknotes. Shorn.

La stella de carta (1947)

Via de li Cappellari

Esce er sole, e la strada è una sparata
de panni de bucata. Appresso, er vento;
ma ar primo capriolo
se trova in un lenzolo
e ce s'addorme drento.

from *Paper Star* (1947)

───────

Via dei Cappellari

The sun comes out and the street's
a carnival of sheets, the wind
right behind. At first leap
it lands in a pillowcase
and falls asleep.

Propaganda

La Luna esce a lo scuro
cor lume a acetilene: sceje er muro,
butta uno sguardo intorno
e senza fa rumore
scrive cor gesso: «Abbasso er Capricorno,»
«Viva l'Orsa Maggiore.»

Propaganda

    At night the moon sneaks into town,
flare in hand, picks a wall,
takes a look around,
and without a sound
writes: *Down with Capricorn,*
Long live Ursa Major.

Lo spauracchio

    Cala le braccia, abbassa la capoccia,
se sdraia in mezzo ar grano;
e li passeri intorno a fa bisboccia.
Un sette ar palandrano, e un senzatetto
trova la paja e je fa er nido in petto.
    Un ber giorno un gricciore
addosso, e un peso qui:
se tocca co la mano, e trova er core.
Strano, invece da batte, fa cì cì.

The Scarecrow

    Head bowed, arms limp at his side,
he lies down in the middle of the field.
Birds fly around him, bold and snide.
His overcoat is torn; a lone sparrow
finds some straw and weaves a lucky burrow.
    One day he feels a shiver in his chest,
fingers around and finds the weight:
right over his heart it comes to rest.
Instead of beating, it goes *tweet!*

Tormarancio (1950)

Quanno è l'ora

Tu lo sai quanno è l'ora, e io t'aspetto:
in petto er core è un sasso.
Buffo, che un regazzino
insegni er primo passo
a un omo. Tu me guardi, e io cammino.

from *Tormarancio* (1950)

When It's Time

     You'll know when it's time.
I'll wait for you, my heart
a millstone in my chest.
Imagine, a boy teaching
a man to walk! You watch
as I take my first baby steps.

Una striscia de sole (1951)

Er teatrino

  Ferma, la pantomina
tra le scene dipinte.
Io pure fermo. A che
serve più er filo, senza la manina
che va e viè tra le quinte?

from *A Strip of Sun* (1951)

───────

Puppet Theater

    The show has stopped
between scenes. I, too,
have stopped. What need
for strings without the hand
to tug them behind the screen?

Er gusto mio (1953)

_____

L'abbete

    Cacciato da la neve,
arriva dar paese
cor cappotto de panno, quello greve.
    E suda tutto l'anno
drento a villa Borghese.

from *How I Like It* (1953)

Spruce

     Hacked from its snowy Eden
it arrives packed
in a burlap sack.
     Year round now it swelters
in the Borghese Gardens.

Er gusto mio

    Sto in campana de dietro a la persiana.
Pare uno scherzo: ma ce vo l'ingegno,
l'occhio e una punta d'estro,
prima de coje ar segno. Io so maestro.
Abbiti ar piano nobbile?
Te sei messo er vestito de la festa?
Smonti da l'automobbile?
    E io te sputo in testa.

How I Like It

    I close the curtain tight so you can't see.
Piece of cake, right? But it's no joke.
You need a trained eye and a bit
of inspiration if you want to hit
your mark. And I'm a master at it.
So you live on the *piano nobile*, dressed
in your Sunday best, well-bred?
Left your Mercedes double-parked?
Too late. My spit lands on your head.

La meridiana

Gnente carica, gnente ticche-tacche:
ma da un secolo e passa che sta ar monno
nun sgarra d'un seconno.
Sempre er sole a le tacche, e segna l'ore
co quer chiodo piantato drento ar core.

Sundial

    No wind-up, no tick-tock,
no key to start. In a century
it hasn't skipped a beat.
    Sunlight turns the hands of this clock,
marks time by the stake at its heart.

Roma 18 poesie (1956)

La scalinata de l'Araceli

Cento scalini (rote
de rondinelle intorno, in gola er core)
e vado in celo. Prima compro un fiore,
così nun me presento a mano vote.

from *Rome 18 Poems* (1956)

The Steps at Aracoeli

    One hundred steps (on every side
a shower of starlings, my heart
lodged in my throat) and I've landed
in heaven. I buy some flowers
so I don't show up empty-handed.

Er cigno (1957)

───────

Luna calante

  Ar collo de la notte era un brelocche:
er Toro, er Capricorno,
l'Orsa Maggiore intorno
e a tant'occhi de foco
a poco a poco s'ariduce a un corno.

from *The Swan* (1957)

Waning Moon

    Diamond 'round the neck of night:
ringed by Taurus, Capricorn,
Ursa Major on the rise—
before so many fiery eyes
bit by bit it's whittled to a horn.

Er girasole

    Giallo su un zeppo verde, teso ar celo
e er respiro sospeso,
un giorno dura er giorno.
    Er sole, manco er sole,
rompe la notte in petto ar girasole.

Sunflower

Bright yellow in a field of green,
face to face with the sky,
holding its breath, calls it a day.
Not even the sun, for all its art,
can purge night from the sunflower's heart.

Omaggio a Esopo (1958)

Diffidenza

Giove compie mill'anni, e l'animali
je porteno er cadò.
La serpe striscia co una rosa in bocca
e Giove: – Cocca, accetto li regali;
ma da una serpe, e da la bocca, no.

from *Homage to Aesop* (1958)

Diffidence

    At Jove's one-thousandth birthday bash
the animals paid their respects.
    The serpent brought a rose. Jove quipped:
"That I love presents everybody knows—
but from a snake, and from its mouth,
that gift I can't accept."

Er consijo de Giove

– È bella l'Appia, e l'aria me s'addice;
ma chi passa me pista –
fiotta er serpente. – Tu
mozzica er primo – dice
Giove – e er seconno nun ce prova più.

Jove's Advice

"I love the Appia, the air is nice,
but everyone who passes
steps on my head," the snake laments.
"Bite the first," Jove counsels,
"the second will think twice."

L'amatore de favole

– Tremila lire, Esopo? Troppo caro! –
e l'amatore sbuffa.
Trova dell'Arco. – Questo, per favore?
–Lei compri Esopo, e poi – dice er libbraro –
questo je lo do a uffa.

The Collector of Fables

"Three-fifty for Aesop? Too much for me!"
the collector cries.
    He finds dell'Arco. "How much for this?"
"Buy Aesop," the bookseller replies,
"I'll throw it in for free."

Natura de li romani

    – Semina ar monno – dice Giove – gola,
ira, accidia, superbia e tutto er resto.
Lesto! – e Mercurio vola.
    Sopra a piazza Colonna
intuzza a la colonna
Antonina, e addio soma!
    Er viaggio, così, finisce a Roma.

Roman Nature

"Go fill the Earth," says Jove,
"with pride, anger, gluttony, sloth,
and every other sin. Now, move!"
And Mercury is off...
In Piazza Colonna, though, he trips,
spills his cargo. What's done is done.
His voyage ends in Rome.

Testa o croce? (1960)

───────

Testa o croce?

    Testa o croce? Lanciata
troppo forte, la luna s'è incollata
a la scialla de pece de la notte
e da lassù te sfotte. Nun saprai
si è testa o croce mai.

from *Heads or Tails?* (1960)

———————

Heads or Tails?

    Heads or tails? Tossed
way too high, the moon got lost
glued to the pitch-black breast of night,
a sleight-of-hand. You'll never know
if it was heads or tails now.

Una cunnola in petto (1961)

Un passo incerto

Un passo incerto e appresso
un passo meno incerto: unita a me,
dentro a me tu cammini.
Prima batteva, adesso
er core è tutto un fruscìo de piedini.

from *A Cradle in My Chest* (1961)

An Unsure Step

    An unsure step, and then
another, less unsure: together
with me—within me—you walk.
    My heart, it used to beat; now, when
I listen, I hear footsteps in the park.

Fermo er respiro

    Fermo er respiro, affonno
un secchio a un pozzo. Invece d'acqua tiro
su una voce dar fonno
e più bevo e più dura
su le labbra l'arsura.

Bated Breath

    With bated breath, I sink my bucket.
No water. Instead, I haul
a voice up from the depths.
The longer I drink, the longer
the burning lasts on the lips.

È sempre giorno

    Finché punti un ditino ar sole, intorno
è sempre giorno e er core
come una meridiana segna l'ore.

Day Lasts Forever

    As long as you point your finger at the sun,
day lasts forever. My heart, a sundial,
marks the hours.

Tutta d'oro

    Tutta d'oro: lo sguardo, le parole,
le carezze perfino.
Sippure nun te vedo, t'indovino
in un raggio de sole
    e ogni raggio de sole esce da me.

All of Gold

    All of gold: your words, your glance,
even your caress.
If I can't make you out, I guess.
In each ray of sun I see
your resemblance:
    each ray of sun originates in me.

Sempre una cunnola

    Sempre sempre una cunnola
dondola dentro a me.
    Come ingrossa lo stormo
de li pensieri e fugge er sonno, canto
«fatte la ninna» e accanto
a te pur io m'addormo.

Always a Cradle

    Always, always a cradle
rocking within me.
    As the swarm of thoughts swells
and sleep slips away
I sing *rock-a-bye,*
and fall asleep, too
right next to you.

Verde vivo verde morto (1962)

Un cono gelato

Tra zabbajone e crema e cioccolato,
scejo er pistacchio e puro
chiuso tra muro e muro,
sospeso er core su un cono gelato,
me succhio a filo a filo d'erba un prato.

from *Living Green Dead Green* (1962)

Ice Cream Cone

    Chocolate, vanilla, or zabaglione?
I go with pistachio, and even though
I'm walled off here alone
I suck up the whole green meadow,
heart balanced on an ice cream cone.

Marziale per un mese (1963)

───────

12.

    M'hai chiesto che me frutta l'orticello.
La fava, no. Er pisello,
no. La scarola, no. Una cosa sola,
Arfredo: a mollo ar verde nun te vedo.

from *Martial for a Month* (1963)

─────────

12.

    You ask how green my garden grows.
No fava beans, no peas, no escarole.
One thing, Alfred, is green:
broke in my garden, *you* can't be seen.

Poesie 1942-1967 (1967)

È matto o nun è matto?

    Er matto, fermo avanti a lo scaffale,
Belli o Trilussa o Pascarella:
quale scejjerà? Quatto-quatto
scejje dell'Arco. Allora nun è matto.

from *Poems 1942-1967* (1967)

Nuts, or Not Nuts?

    He's been at the bookshelf for hours, that putz,
with Belli, Trilussa, Pascarella:
which will he pick? Dell'Arco, that old fox!
I guess he isn't nuts.

Vino e poesia

    Insieme ar libbro mio
er vino mio t'ho dato.
«Nun me lo firmi?» e io
t'ho firmato la boccia de moscato.

Wine and Poetry

    I hand you a copy of my book
with a bottle of wine. *Signed?*
says your look. I sign
the bottle. The label's mine.

Ho arzato un muro

È mia la corpa. Ho arzato
a sasso a sasso a sasso
tra me e la gente un muro.
Gnente da fa. Sippuro
te vojjo dà la mano, ar primo passo
sbatto co la capoccia addosso ar muro.

I Built a Wall

      It's my fault. Stone by stone
by stone I built a wall,
walled myself off from the world.
      No way out now.
Even if I wanted to
feel your hand, one
step and I'd crack
my head on that wall.

E bevo fiori e vino (1968)

Er vino de Genzano

I.

    Come sbarco a Genzano
a la prima oseteria,
a fojetta a fojetta abbrucio l'ore.
    Forte in bocca è l'odore der trebbiano
e me la sciacquo co la marvasia.

II.

    Come un celo ingrugnato la capoccia,
ogni pensiero un nuvolone nero.
    Bevo un bicchier de vino
fino all'urtima goccia
e er celo se colora de turchino.

III.

    Più ammucchi l'oro ne la botte e più
arzi fra te e la gente un muro, tu.

from *And I Drink Flowers and Wine* (1968)

Genzano Wine

I.

    The minute I'm in Genzano,
carafe by carafe, I burn the hours
at the first tavern I find. Strong
    is the bouquet of *trebbiano*;
I wash it down with *malvasia*.

II.

    My head is an impenetrable sky,
each thought a darkening cloud.
    I empty a glass of wine
to the final drop, and suddenly
blue skies open up.

III.

    The more you fill the bottle up with gold
the higher the wall between you and the world.

Dentro a la botte mia
freme la marvasia
e finché butta ogni bucale
frutta un amico de più.

IV.

Un bucale per omo
brinato da la grotta e nun se sciupi
manco una goccia!
Er gotto pieno in mano,
io t'offro l'occasione d'èsse omo.
Come sfuma l'effetto der trebbiano
tornamo – l'uno azzanna l'artro – lupi.

V.

Hai stappato la boccia
e sversi lo sciampagna a goccia a goccia
in un bicchiere de cristallo. Pietro,
damme er genzano in un bicchier de vetro.

VI.

Io sacrifico er vino ar dio der vino.
Cesanese color de la viola:
amatista tritata e raspa in gola.
Spunta a ogni gotto un'artra penna all'ale,

Deep in my bottle
the *malvasia* bubbles
and till my pitcher ends,
I count a loyal friend.

IV.

A pitcher for each man,
iced in the cellar—and don't you dare
squander a single drop!
Full chalice in hand, I offer you
this chance to be a man.
As soon as the *trebbiano* wears off
we're at each other's throats again.

V.

Bottle uncorked, you pour
champagne, drop by precious drop,
into a crystal goblet. Pietro,
bring me *genzano* in a water cup.

VI.

I sacrifice wine to the god of wine,
violet-colored *cesanese*,
crushed amethyst that burns the throat.
With every glass another feather sprouts

un'artra spinta in celo a ogni bucale.
Un trono, una grillanna
de fronne d'uva: e ciuccia
ar vetro, ciuccia a la bocca d'Arianna,
dio der vino so' io.

VII.

   Una ventata spalla l'Infiorata
e dar tinello de via Livia cola
colore der rubbino
una marrana: a galla
er petalo de rosa, de viola,
de garofolo e bevo fiori e vino.

VIII.

   Logro un'ora, dua, tre
davanti ar gotto. Er vino
cala ner vetro, cresce dentro a me
la notte e me strascino,
l'occhi pieni de sonno, for dar monno.

IX.

   Su la vigna sfarfalla
l'urtima fronna gialla.
Bevo – e la vite torna verde, er pampano

on my wings, heaven grows kinder.
A throne, a garland
of vine-leaves: as you suckle
the glass, you suck Ariadne's kiss.
The god of wine is me.

VII.

    A gust of wind ruffles the Infiorata
and into the tavern on Via Livia
flows a ruby-colored stream
of petals: rose, violet, and clove, afloat.
And I drink flowers and wine.

VIII.

    I while away an hour, two, three
in front of my glass. As the wine
drains from the bottle, night lengthens
inside me. I drag myself,
sleepy-eyed, out of this world.

IX.

    The last yellow leaves
flutter on the vine.
I drink and it goes green again,

ar primo guizzo tocca er celo.
    Bevo – e er cesanese
torna rampazzo d'uva, torna
sugo de sole in bocca.

X.

    Terra a l'orecchie – eppure da lontano
sento er mosto che sgoccia dentro ar tino.
All'occhi terra – eppure vedo er vino,
er primo vino e sia
cesanese o trebbiano o marvasia,
vince in bocca er sapore de la terra.

shoots straight up to the sky.
    I drink and the wine
becomes a bunch of grapes, becomes
liquid sun in my mouth.

X.

    Earth, up to my ears—yet from afar
I hear the must in the tub as it drips.
Earth, up to my eyes—yet I see the wine,
the new wine, and it makes no difference—
cesanese, *trebbiano*, or *malvasia*—
the taste of earth prevails and seals my lips.

Tiber River Anthology (1970)

IV.

Io dott. e prof. e libbero docente,
socio corrispondente
e accademico insigne de... e de... e de...
L'unico sbajo curamme da me.

from *Tiber River Anthology* (1970)

_____

IV.

    I, Dr., Prof., freelance docent,
full-partner, correspondent,
academic luminary of this and that...
    Cause of death? I put on my physician's hat.

X.

QUI (finarmente!) GIACE
IN PACE (lui e er cliente, tutt'e dua)
STRAPPAPELO BARBIERE (Terra, mai
greve e fredda sarai come la mano sua).

X.

HERE (at last!) LIES
HAIRPULLER THE BARBER (together
with his client) R.I.P. (Earth, cold and vulgar,
is far more soothing than his hand of ice.)

XI.

A la fine er Signore s'è riccorto
Teodoro beccamorto.
Zappa e pala ar lavoro
armeno mezzo secolo: percui
è giusto che riposi puro lui.

XI.

    At last God has recalled
the gravedigger Theodore
    who shoveled, hoed, and hauled
a half-century or more with zest.
Now he deserves a rest.

XVI.

Crollati li confini
de piazza Montanara, li burrini
so' mijara e mijara de mijara.
  Inutile, sor coso,
che sventoli er baiocco,
indeciso tra er 'fiocco'
e la 'cicia'! Santaccia oggi è a riposo.

XVI.

    The walls have fallen in around
Piazza Montanara, and now
yokels by the score abound.
    Mr. Whatever-your-name-is, waving
your wallet, unsure which you want
more—her asshole or her cunt—
put your money away. Santaccia's off today.

Caccia sì caccia no (1971)

———

Un trillo dentro a me

    L'occhio fisso ar mirino,
ramo a ramo smucìno
tutto l'ormo finché m'accorgo che,
fringuello o rosignolo o cardellino,
er trillo è dentro a me.

from *Hunting Diary* (1971)

A Trill Within

    Eye fixed to the scope,
branch by branch, I pick apart
the entire elm. And what do you know?
Cardinal or nightingale or sparrow,
the trill is in my heart.

Er beccafico

Pijo la mira e sparo:
ma prima d'ariccoje er beccafico
me capo tra le foje
(la goccia a pennolone
e la coccia viola
co li sgraffi d'argento) er mejo fico.
È buffo: in bocca è amaro.

Warbler

    I take my aim and shoot:
before the bird is mine
I pluck from between the leaves
the finest fig (hung
like a raindrop, its violet skin
streaked silver). Funny,
    it's bitter on the tongue.

Una bella morte

Intinto ar verde, er becco
pieno de porpa inzuccherata, ecco,
dico, una bella morte.
Ogni scrupolo è vinto
e sparo ar beccafico.

A Beautiful Death

The warbler tears at the fig, his beak
smeared with sugary pulp.
I think, *A beautiful death.*
I force a gulp, pull
the trigger and steal his breath.

Lasciatemi divertire,

ovvero Marziale per un altro mese (1972)

6.

    Cento scrocconi a cena
intorno a Giggi, e m'è arrivato appena
er fumo de le pile. Affumicato
e a panza vòta, io
tra cento schiavi me so' inteso un dio.

from *Let Me Have Some Fun,*

or Martial for Another Month (1972)

6.

    A hundred flatterers hawk around Katz's
table, and for me nothing
but fumes from the kitchen.
Smoked like a sturgeon, kishkes
empty, among a hundred beggars, I'm a king.

8.

Sempre nature morte:
oggi ha dipinto un pollo. Scellerato!
L'ha ammazzato du' vorte.

8.

Again painting still lifes:
today, a chicken. Evil man!
Murdered the damn thing twice.

15.

So' brutti o belli st'epigrammi? Boooh!
Oggi l'ho chiesto a te,
amico svisciolato, e scartabbelli
tra le paggine, e aggricci er naso, e
me fai segno de no.
Ho capito: so' belli.

15.

    Are these epigrams any good? Who knows?
I asked you, dear dedicated friend,
and you leafed through them page
by page, wrinkling up your nose,
shaking your head, *no*.
    They're excellent—that's how I know.

23.

    Te sbrodoli de sugo e besciamella
e panna, e poi borbotti
contro chi t'ha sfamato. Gi', è una iella
    èsse orgojosi e jotti.

23.

    You fress like a hog—loud, face smeared
in fancy sauces, yet have the chutzpah
to insult while you gorge. Moish', it's bad
    karma to be both gluttonous and proud.

26.

Una coppia de tordi
strappati ar ramo da lo schioppo, er guizzo
d'argento d'una tinca presa all'amo:
caccia e pesca è un festino da milordi.
　　Vecchio ero a Roma. Qui
m'intosta l'aria, er vino
m'accenne er sangue. Un'artra piazza ar letto
e aspetto una regazza
che me dica de sì.

26.

    A pair of thrushes picked
off the branch, the glint
of a hooked tench, I hunt
and fish like a lord—to my heart's content.
    In Rome, I was old. Here
crisp air emboldens,
wine heats my blood. Toss
another pillow on the mattress,
I'll wait right here for the girl who says *yes*.

A li quattro cantoni (1973)

───────

Er pesce anarfabbeta

Er silabbario casca ne l'acquario.
Er pesce anarfabbeta
sfugge all'*emme* e a la *bi*,
schiva l'*acca* e la *pi*:
ma resta preso all'amo de la *zeta*.

from *Four Corners* (1973)

The Illiterate Fish

    Someone dropped a grammar book
in an aquarium. The fish,
illiterate, darted away
from *m* and *b*, zig-
zagged around *h* and *p*
but in the end the *z*
snagged it on a hook.

A caccia

Macché tordo, macché
quaja, macché beccaccia!
Vado a caccia de stelle.
Basta un retino da farfalle – e
indeciso tra Orione
e Vega e lo Scorpione,
m'affiaro su Boòte.
All'arba m'aritrovo a mano vote
e er retino bruciato.

Star Hunter

    Forget about thrushes, quails,
woodcocks! I'm out hunting
stars with a butterfly net.
Undecided between Orion,
Vega, and Scorpio, I bet
on the Herdsman, Boötes.
    At dawn I return empty-handed,
net burnt to a crisp.

Una fetta de cocommero

    La bocca fa la spola
ancora ne la porpa (er gelo in gola,
er foco su la faccia) e ancora intatta
la fetta de cocommero.
E l'estate d'allora dura ancora.

A Slice of Watermelon

    Back and forth, teeth
saw though its pulp (freeze
in the throat, face burned)
and still it's intact. Lost days
of summers long ago return.

Ombra più ombra (1974)

———

Come una lepre

    Come una lepre, via tra spica e spica
e l'ombra una fatica a stamme appresso.
Un passo fiacco adesso:
adesso un passo corto
e l'ombra un peso morto.

from *Shadowplay* (1974)

Like a Hare

A hare, I scamper through the wheat.
My shadow can't keep up. It's beat.
A slower step, and now
a shorter one, my shadow—
a ball and chain at my feet.

Poesie 1950–1975 (1976)

Fronne morte

    A ogni ventata c'è,
forte, sempre più forte, una cascata
de fronne morte.
    Quercia, pioppo, ormo:
nessun arbero intorno.
Le fronne morte cascheno da me.

from *Poems 1950–1975* (1976)

Dead Branches

    Each gust of wind
gathers force, throws down
an avalanche of branches.
    Oak, poplar, elm:
no trees around.
In me they fall, dead weight and all.

Arciroma (1978)

Er Colosseo è una conchija

  Inutile che accosti ar Colosseo
l'orecchia, amico mio.
  L'urlo der gladiatore vincitore,
li zoccoli der toro,
er fiotto der Tedeo,
la musica der coro:
è robba che la sento solo io.

from *Arciroma* (1978)

―――――

The Colosseum Is a Shell

  Forget about putting your ear
to the Colosseum, friend.
  The gladiator's winning cry,
the bulls' stampede,
the music of the choir,
the whining *Te Deum*. In the end
it's noise I alone can hear.

Tomba de Nerone

    Affacciato a la tomba,
rossa la barba, rossa
la chioma – e la ghitarra a pennolone,
nun c'è dubbio: è Nerone
e la voce rimbomba.
    «Ho sbajato» confessa «e me ne pento.
Oggi, è er momento de dà foco a Roma».

Nero's Tomb

He stands before the tomb:
red beard, red tresses, dangling
guitar. Nero, no doubt.
His voice thunders down:
   "I screwed up," he confesses, "and repent—
now is the time to burn Rome to the ground!"

Er cocommero

Una cortella addosso
a un cocommero – e tanti,
tanti spicchi de luna
ner celo verde de la bancarella.
Un chiar de luna rosso.

Watermelon

    A man carves watermelons
beneath the green shade
of the vendor's stand.
Dozens of half-moons
    make moonlight red.

Basta (o no?)

    Dico: basta! Ho strappato
er fojetto de carta
tutto scarabbozzato,
ho rotto in dua la penna – e porto in petto
(un peso morto), sia
brutta, sia bella, l'urtima poesia.

Enough (or Not?)

Enough! I've shredded
this scribbled-up page, snapped
my pen in half
and carry—like deadweight in my chest—
worthy or not
this poem, my last.

Gatti (1980)

Io, gatto

    Una crosta de rogna
e uno stormo de purce in mezzo ar pelo:
nessuno me s'accosta.
Sia a galla all'erba, sia
sdraiato sur serciato,
m'imbriaco de sole.
A tempo perso dormo
e in sogno, verso a verso,
sgnàvolo una poesia.

from *Cats* (1980)

―――

I, Cat

    Scabs on my back,
ransacked by fleas,
no one approaches.
I laze on the grass, stretch
across the sidewalk,
stoned on sunlight.
Nothing to do, I drowse.
In my dreams, verse
by verse, a poem meows.

Flora (1981)

La mela

   È rimasta una mela tra le foje
de la rama più arta: è la più bella.
Sfuggita a chi le coje,
me dispiace ma a quella
ciarrivo solo io.

from *Flora* (1981)

The Apple

One last apple among the leaves
of the highest branch, the sweetest.
The pickers must've missed it.
No matter—only I
can reach that high.

Assolo (1982)

Assolo

     Arsura – e manco un sorso
de celo. Intorno
er sonno de le foje
e in pieno giorno cola
un silenzio sur monno.
     Eppure tra noi dua nasce un discorso.
Un filo d'erba nato in bocca – e
er prato dentro a me: la filastrocca
de la cicala, er volo
d'un rosignolo, er guizzo d'un ramarro.
De punto in bianco, morto er prato, secco
er filo d'erba in bocca.
     Cammino a testa bassa sur serciato
e svìcolo perfino
dar turchino specchiato ner pantano.
Intorno a me, er deserto
me lega mejo a te.
     L'impronta mia è rimasta su la rena,
vicino a quella tua.
È strano. Sia l'ondata d'acqua, sia
la ventata: nessuno la scancella.
In riva ar lago semo sempre in dua.
     Sopra ar fojetto, bianco
su bianco, scrivo a te.

from *Solo* (1982)

Solo

    Scorching heat—not so much as a drop
from the sky. All around
the sleep of leaves,
and right in the middle of the day
silence falls like a knell.
    Yet our conversation has begun.
A blade of grass in the mouth, a meadow
in my blood: the cicada's song,
a nightingale's flight, a lizard's flash.
Then, without warning, the meadow's wilted,
the blade dry in my mouth.
    Head bowed, I schlep down the street
sidestepping even
the mirrored blue of puddles.
The desert around me binds me
more tightly to you.
    My footprint—there it is on the sand
right next to yours.
Strange. Neither waves nor wind
can delete it.
Here by the lake, we're always two of us.
    A blank page, white on white,
I write to you.
Not even a pause, and on

Manco una sosta – e
su l'istesso fojetto,
bianco su bianco, leggo la risposta.
　Un celo annuvolato
ma nasceva da te
una striscia de sole. Intatto er prato,
un turchino lassù senza una nuvola:
ma la striscia de sole nun c'è più.
　Muto o pieno de trilli er celo: chiaro
o soffocato da la nebbia, è
sempre notte pe me.
Cammino in un ghiacciaro
de marmo: unica luce un'ombra, tu.
　Secco sotto a uno stormo
de fronne secche hanno tajato l'ormo.
Sparito er tronco in riva ar prato, l'ombra
è rimasta sull'erba e fermo all'ombra
dell'ormo morto te ritrovo viva.
Uscita a spasso – e
er rumore der passo
ogni giorno me chiama: ma a che vale
corre lungo er viale?
Cammini dentro a me.
　Una parola – una parola sola,
l'urtima ieri: un sorso
d'amore asciutto su le labbra. È
oggi un discorso muto
tutto diretto a me.
　La notte è scesa su
una lastra de marmo, su un cipresso.
Pesa er silenzio intorno
ma pe noi (un'ombra tu,
un'ombra io) comincia adesso er giorno.
　Pieno er celo de nuvole o sereno,

the same blank page—white
on white—your answer, in your hand.
    Sky overcast, yet a glimmer
of light appeared with you.
With it the meadow, the cloudless blue.
The glimmer's gone now.
    The sky, be it loud with birds or silent,
starlit or strangled by fog,
for me it's always night.
I walk inside a marble glacier,
your shadow my only light.
    The parched elm, swarmed by dry
branches, was felled. Its trunk
has vanished from the field,
though its shadow endures on the grass.
Motionless, I find you there
in the shade of the felled elm, alive.
You went out for a stroll, and still
the sound of your footsteps
haunts me. To what end
do I rush down the street?
You stroll inside of me.
    Yesterday, a word—a single word,
the last. The dry taste
of love on the lips. Today
our conversation is mute. It's just
me now talking to me.
    Night falls across
a slab of marble, a cypress.
Silence is manifest,
but for us (you a shade,
me a shade) day begins today.
    Cloudy or clear, it doesn't matter.
My feet follow the path

diretto er passo mio
verso er lago. Specchiata,
incantata ner lago
nun te spezzi nemmeno
si tiro in acqua un sasso.
 Una voce turchina:
voce de mare dentro a una conchija
in un velo de spuma.
Sempre viva bisbija
una voce turchina
oggi a l'orecchia mia: voce de celo.
 Morta solo una vorta
e addosso er gelo, tu.
Sempre più solo, sempre più sperduto,
ogni giorno ritorno
scosso dar gelo – e mòro
vicino a te ogni giorno.
 Troppo in ritardo l'urtimo
giorno: troppo lontano.
Slunghi una mano tu
in quer giorno, me tocchi:
una carezza appena – e chiudo l'occhi.
Doppo, a lo scuro, nun me lasci più.

straight to the lake. Reflected,
enchanted on its surface,
your image won't shatter—
not even if I skip a stone across the water.
    A blue voice,
the sea's voice deep within a shell
caught in the surf's veil.
Always alive, it whispers
its blue in my ear:
the voice of the sky.
    Dead, you're frozen
forever. Ever more alone,
ever more lost,
every day I return
jarred by the chill and die
each day by your side.
    The last day arrives too late.
It's far too far away.
On that day you reach for me—
just a caress. I shut
my eyes. In darkness, then,
I'm certain you'll never leave me again.

Gatti, e chi vuole gatti? (1985)

Er gatto de cennere

A poco a poco s'è lograto er foco.
Su li rocchi de legna,
capoccia, e groppa, e coda
sboccia un gatto de cennere,
ancora accese du' faville: l'occhi.

from *Cats, Who Wants Cats?* (1985)

The Ash-Cat

    Bit by bit the fire's gone cold
but from smoking embers
head, back, and tail unfold
from ash: a cat. Its eyes—
two quick sparks—still smolder.

Er gatto color sabbia

    Nessuna meravija
si er gatto color sabbia
ammassa in corpo rabbia.
    Qualunque pupo passa
allunga la manina – e je smucina
er pelo finché trova la conchija.

The Sand-Colored Cat

    No wonder
the sand-colored cat
is mad as hell.
    Every boy who walks past
rummages through its fur
until he finds a shell.

Vince er turchino (1985)

Paura d'èsse solo

Paura d'èsse solo.
Invento un'osteria – e pesco a volo
un amico: un amico
pronto a divide (spero)
un pensiero sereno.
Odor de vino – e
a la salute! dico:
ma er tavolino è vòto avanti a me,
in mano a me er bicchiere resta pieno.

from *Triumph of Blue* (1985)

Fear of Solitude

  Fear of solitude.
I dream up a bistrot, a friend—
a willing companion (I hope)
to share my conversation.
  The scent of wine—I stand
for a toast. "To your health!"
But the table's set for one,
the cup still full in my hand.

Passo ponte (1986)

Una pannocchia de stelle

Luce in faccia e calore su la pelle
in mano a me matura una pannocchia
fitta fitta de stelle.
L'unica scocciatura
sgranalla a primasera dar Giannicolo
dentro a la cappa nera.

from *Crossing the Bridge* (1986)

A Cob Thick with Stars

    Light on my face, heat on my skin,
a cob of corn thick with stars
ripens in my hands.
    But here's the task:
at dusk, from the Janiculum,
to pluck them out of the dark.

L'angelo disparo (1990)

Campo de Fiori

    Campo de Fiori – e ferma sur mercato
la puzza de bruciato.
    Fruttarolo, orzarolo,
pesciarolo: nessuno
ne sa gnente. A lo scuro
puro Giordano Bruno.

from *Odd-Numbered Angel* (1990)

Campo de' Fiori

  Campo de' Fiori—a burning smell
hovers above the stalls.
  Fishmonger, fruit seller,
nut vendor—who lit the spark?
Even Giordano Bruno's in the dark.

Roma Romae (1991)

Er merlo

    Nero come er carbone
la notte se l'ignotte in un boccone.
    A mollo ar nero fino ar collo, er becco
(un petalo de sole) bussa ar celo:
er celo s'apre – e sorte un sole intero.

from *Roma Romae* (1991)

Blackbird

    Black as coal,
night swallows it whole.
    Drowning in darkness, its beak
(a fleck of light) pecks at the sky: *tin,*
tin. It opens—sunlight comes roaring in.

Scala a lumaca

    A pesca d'un turchino
rugante, senza er velo d'una nuvola,
a scalino a scalino
finito er girotonno
esco dar monno e casco dritto in celo.

Spiral Staircase

In search of a bawdy shade
of blue, without the slightest wisp of cloud,
stair by stair I ascend.
I've stumbled, by spiral's end,
out of this world and into heaven.

Notes to the Poems

Sloth: This poem functions as a kind of ars poetica. According to Marcello Fagiolo dell'Arco, the poet's son, it was written while the family was living "in forced exile" in Umbria, having left Rome because of the war. It was there dell'Arco wrote: "No more sonnets. Concise poems, almost epigrams. A nest-egg of verses."

Tasso's Oak: The poet Torquato Tasso (1544–1595) is said to have enjoyed the shade of this oak tree, whose position on Rome's Janiculum offers a spectacular view of the city. After being struck by lightning, it is now a charred remnant. Also the subject of a poem by Trilussa.

Via dei Cappellari: On this narrow street near Campo de' Fiori, one may still see the occasional clothesline strung between facing windows.

The Steps at Aracoeli: Santa Maria in Aracoeli (Latin for "altar of heaven"), adjacent to the Campidoglio—Rome's centermost point—is a church located at the top of an enormous staircase.

Jove Counsels: Via Appia Antica is a Roman road leading south to Brindisi. It was—and is—a popular spot for a Sunday stroll, lined with umbrella pines and ancient monuments.

Roman Nature: Piazza Colonna, named for the Column of Marcus Aurelius at its center, is also home to Montecitorio, the Italian Parliament.

A Cradle in My Chest: Dell'Arco's dedication to this book of poems reads, "For my unborn daughter."

Ice Cream Cone: Zabaglione, a treat made from egg yolk, sugar, and Marsala wine, has four syllables and nearly end-rhymes with *say* and *gray*.

Martial for a Month: Dell'Arco published three books of loose translations from the Latin poets Martial, Catullus, and Horace. His versions are fully realized dell'Arco poems, and as he states explicitly in the title of *Let Me Have Some Fun*—his second book of Martial translations—these are not meant to be accurate or scholarly renderings of classical verse. My hope is that something of dell'Arco's—and Martial's—astringent humor shines through.

Genzano Wine: Genzano is one of the Roman Castles, a group of towns located to the south of Rome known for their wine. Dell'Arco relocated to Genzano, his father's hometown, in the 1960s. During the Infiorata festival, streets are painstakingly decorated with elaborate, colorful patterns of flower petals in honor of the festival of Corpus Christi. The festival takes place on Via Livia.

Tiber River Anthology: After Edgar Lee Masters' *Spoon River Anthology*. Santaccia is the infamous prostitute of Belli lore, who plied her trade in Piazza Montanara. Once located between the Theater of Marcellus and the Campidoglio, the square was demolished during the Fascist period. In keeping with Belli, whose two sonnets about Santaccia are felicitously obscene, I have tried to avoid the advice of my better angels to sanitize the language in dell'Arco's vignette. (In his sonnet "The Mother of the Saints" [1832], Belli makes a list of all the euphemisms for "vagina" that will fit in a 14-line poem, among them *cicia*—the same term that appears in dell'Arco's poem.)

Nero's Tomb: The Great Fire of Rome occurred in 64 CE. Legend has it that the Emperor Nero played his lyre—or flute, or fiddle, or in this case guitar—as he watched the city burn. Legend also has it that Nero's tomb is located in northern Rome, though the tomb in question is not actually his.

Watermelons: Anyone who knows Rome knows the summer watermelon vendors whose cry of "Taja ch'è rosso!" gave dell'Arco the title of his first book. The phrase is an invitation to taste the ripe red fruit, or—in the case of Mario dell'Arco—to read his poems.

Solo: Written after the death of the poet's wife Anna Maria in 1978.

A Cob Thick with Stars: The Janiculum is the highest of Rome's hills, though not one of the "seven hills of Rome."

Campo de' Fiori: This is the square where the philosopher Giordano Bruno (1548–1600) was burned alive by the Catholic Church for his heretical opinions. Today, a statue of Bruno stands at the center of this bustling Roman market.

Spiral Staircase: This poem likely refers to the spiral staircase leading to the top of the dome of St. Peter's in Rome—a vertiginous ascent.

Acknowledgments

I am grateful to Marcello Fagiolo dell'Arco for granting me permission to translate his father's words, as well as to Carolina Marconi and Gangemi Editore for their blessings and encouragement. I am indebted to Michael Palma, without whose support this project may never have been more than a handful of far-flung translations scattered around the Internet. Thanks also to Alexander Booth for proofreading this manuscript and offering many useful suggestions, and to Mike Stocks for showing me the way with his Belli translations. My deepest gratitude goes to Matvei Yankelevich, Donna Masini, and the folks at World Poetry Books for offering this wayward project a home.

I have made use of various resources, the most valuable of which are my own Roman relatives whose spoken language bears more than a passing resemblance to that of Mario dell'Arco's poetry. Romanesco is less a dialect today than an attitude, and living among Romans is the best way to absorb it. I have made use of Fernando Ravaro's copious *Dizionario Romanesco* (Newton Compton, 1996) as well as the various glossaries and notes in the editions of Belli, Trilussa, and dell'Arco at my disposal. The poems, as well as the biographical information in the introduction, are from *Tutte le poesie romanesche* (Gangemi, 2005). For further context I have consulted the volume *Studi su Mario dell'Arco* (Gangemi, 2006).

Some of the translations in this book previously appeared in the following journals: *Journal of Italian Translation*, *First Things*, *On the Seawall*, *One Art*, *Los Angeles Review*, *Packingtown Review*, *Asses of Parnassus*, *Italian Americana*, *Bad Lilies*, and *THINK*. My thanks to the editors for their generosity of spirit.

Mario dell'Arco, circa 1945. Courtesy of Fondo Mario dell'Arco.

Mario dell'Arco, the pen name of Mario Fagiolo (Rome, 1905–1996), was the most significant Romanesco poet of the latter half of the twentieth century. An architect by profession, he abandoned architecture for poetry after World War II. He published nearly 60 books and chapbooks of poetry in his lifetime. His work is marked by its bittersweet, almost jaded stance, a hallmark of the Roman attitude towards life (and death).

Marc Alan Di Martino is the author of the collections *Love Poem with Pomegranate* (Ghost City Press), *Still Life with City* (Pski's Porch), and *Unburial* (Kelsay). His poems and translations appear in *Bad Lilies*, *Palette*, *Rattle*, and many other journals and anthologies. His work has been nominated for both the Pushcart Prize and Best of the Net. He lives in Perugia, Italy.

This book was typeset in Zenon, a contemporary roman developed from analysis of Renaissance models. It was designed by Riccardo Olocco from 2013 to 2022 for Cooperativa Anonima Servizi Tipografici, Verona. The artwork on the cover is a work by Renato Guttuso (1911–1987), an Italian painter considered to be one of the key figures of Italian expressionism. In 1940, Guttuso joined the (then clandestine) Italian Communist Party and later served twice as its representative to the Senate of the Republic. The portrait of the author used as a frontispiece is by Eugen Drăguțescu (1914–1993), a Romanian artist who settled in Rome in 1959; it is reproduced here with the kind permission Marcello Fagiolo dell'Arco and Fondo Mario dell'Arco. Cover design by Andrew Bourne. Typesetting by Don't Look Now. Printed and bound by BALTO Print in Lithuania.

 WORLD POETRY

Marie-Noëlle Agniau
The Escapades
tr. Jesse Hover Amar

Jean-Paul Auxeméry
Selected Poems
tr. Nathaniel Tarn

Boethius
The Poems from On the Consolation of Philosophy
tr. Peter Glassgold

Maria Borio
Transparencies
tr. Danielle Pieratti

Jeannette L. Clariond
Goddesses of Water
tr. Samantha Schnee

Jacques Darras
John Scotus Eriugena at Laon
tr. Richard Sieburth

Mario dell'Arco
Day Lasts Forever: Selected Poems
tr. Marc Alan Di Martino

Marie de Quatrebarbes
The Vitals
tr. Aiden Farrell

Olivia Elias
Chaos, Crossing
tr. Kareem James Abu-Zeid

Gastón Fernández
Apparent Breviary
tr. KM Cascia

Jerzy Ficowski
Everything I Don't Know
tr. Jennifer Grotz & Piotr Sommer
PEN AWARD FOR POETRY IN TRANSLATION

Antonio Gamoneda
Book of the Cold
tr. Katherine M. Hedeen & Víctor Rodríguez Núñez

Mireille Gansel
Soul House
tr. Joan Seliger Sidney

Óscar García Sierra
Houston, I'm the problem
tr. Carmen Yus Quintero

Phoebe Giannisi
Homerica
tr. Brian Sneeden

Zuzanna Ginczanka
On Centaurs & Other Poems
tr. Alex Braslavsky

Julien Gracq
Abounding Freedom
tr. Alice Yang

Leeladhar Jagoori
What of the Earth Was Saved
tr. Matt Reeck

Nakedness Is My End: Poems from the Greek Anthology
tr. Edmund Keeley

Jazra Khaleed
The Light That Burns Us
ed. Karen Van Dyck

Judith Kiros
O
tr. Kira Josefsson

Dimitra Kotoula
The Slow Horizon That Breathes
tr. Maria Nazos

Maria Laina
Hers
tr. Karen Van Dyck

Maria Laina
Rose Fear
tr. Sarah McCann

Perrin Langda
A Few Microseconds on Earth
tr. Pauline Levy Valensi

Afrizal Malna
Document Shredding Museum
tr. Daniel Owen

Joyce Mansour
In the Glittering Maw: Selected Poems
tr. C. Francis Fisher

Manuel Maples Arce
Stridentist Poems
tr. KM Cascia

Ennio Moltedo
Night
tr. Marguerite Feitlowitz

Meret Oppenheim
The Loveliest Vowel Empties: Collected Poems
tr. Kathleen Heil

Giovanni Pascoli
Last Dream
tr. Geoffrey Brock
RAIZISS/DE PALCHI TRANSLATION AWARD

Gabriel Pomerand
Saint Ghetto of the Loans
tr. Michael Kasper &
Bhamati Viswanathan

Liliana Ponce
Theory of the Voice and Dream
tr. Michael Martin Shea

Rainer Maria Rilke
Where the Paths Do Not Go
tr. Burton Pike

Amelia Rosselli
Document
tr. Roberta Antognini & Deborah Woodard

Elisabeth Rynell
Night Talks
tr. Rika Lesser

Waly Salomão
Border Fare
tr. Maryam Monalisa Gharavi

George Sarantaris
Abyss and Song: Selected Poems
tr. Pria Louka

George Seferis
Book of Exercises II
tr. Jennifer R. Kellogg

Seo Jung Hak
The Cheapest France in Town
tr. Megan Sungyoon

Ardengo Soffici
Simultaneities & Lyric Chemisms
tr. Olivia E. Sears

Paul Verlaine
Before Wisdom: The Early Poems
tr. Keith Waldrop & K.A. Hays

Witold Wirpsza
Apotheosis of Music
tr. Frank L. Vigoda

Uljana Wolf
kochanie, today i bought bread
tr. Greg Nissan

Ye LIJun
My Mountain Country
tr. Fiona Sze-Lorrain

Verónica Zondek
Cold Fire
tr. Katherine Silver